MEET THE GREATS

Pope
Francis

TIM COOKE

Gareth Stevens
PUBLISHING

Please visit our website, www.garethstevens.com. For a free color catalog of all our high-quality books, call toll free 1-800-542-2595 or fax 1-877-542-2596.

Cataloging-in-Publication Data

Names: Cooke, Tim.
Title: Pope Francis / Tim Cooke.
Description: New York : Gareth Stevens Publishing, 2019. | Series: Meet the greats | Includes glossary and index.
Identifiers: LCCN ISBN 9781538225769 (pbk.) | ISBN 9781538225752 (library bound)
Subjects: LCSH: Francis, Pope, 1936–Juvenile literature. | Popes–Biography–Juvenile literature.
Classification: LCC BX1378.7 C66 2019 | DDC 282.092 B–dc23

Published in 2019 by
Gareth Stevens Publishing
111 East 14th Street, Suite 349
New York, NY 10003

For Brown Bear Books Ltd:
Editorial Director: Lindsey Lowe
Managing Editor: Tim Cooke
Children's Publisher: Anne O'Daly
Design Manager: Keith Davis
Designer and illustrator: Supriya Sahai
Picture Manager: Sophie Mortimer

Concept development: Square and Circus / Brown Bear Books Ltd

Picture Credits: Front Cover: Character artwork, Supriya Sahai. Interior: Alamy: Keystone Pictures USA, 18; AP: 8, 40, Michael Sohn, 41, Pablo Martinez Monsivais, 43; Catholic World: 34b; Dreamstime: Awizard, 14b, Photogolfer 35t; Getty Images: AFP, 9, AFP/Filippo Monteforte, 42, API/GAMMA, 13, Derrick Ceyrac, 32, EPA, 29, Joe Raedle, 35b; iStock: Zu_09, 38; La Croix: 22, 28b; Public Domain: Archivo de la Nacion Argentino, 10, Argentine Football Association, 30, Dnalov01, 32, Jesuits USA, 15t, Beatrice Murch, 25t, Osservatore Romano, 23t, 23b, WikiLaurent, 20; Robert Hunt Library: 11, 12, 15b, 19; Shutterstock: sunsinger, 33; Thinkstock: adisa, 39; Topfoto: Ullsteinbild, 21, 24b, 25b.

Character artwork © Supriya Sahai
All other artworks Brown Bear Books Ltd

Brown Bear Books has made every attempt to contact the copyright holders.
If anyone has any information please contact licensing@brownbearbooks.co.uk

CPSIA compliance information: Batch #CS18GS. For further information contact Gareth Stevens, New York, New York at 1-800-542-2595.

Contents

Introduction

Growing up in Argentina, Pope Francis knew from the age of 16 that he wanted to be a priest and help people.

*F*rancis's real name was Jorge. He was a smart boy who loved soccer and science. When he became a priest, he had his own ideas about how the Catholic church should behave. Throughout his career, Francis has always tried to help the poor and disadvantaged. When he became the first pope from the Americas in 2013, Francis refused to accept the luxuries that went with the **papal** office, such as a huge residence in the Vatican. Instead, he chose to live in a simple two-bedroom apartment.

Francis's career has been marked by **controversy**. He worked in Argentina at a time when the country's military government had its political opponents killed. Francis worked with the government despite being criticized for doing so. As pope, his support of gay and divorced people offended traditional Catholics. Among most Catholics, however, he is popular and admired.

Argentine UPBRINGING

Jorge Mario Bergoglio was born into a family of Italian immigrants in Buenos Aires, Argentina. No one imagined he might one day become pope.

Jorge was born on December 17, 1936. He was the eldest of five children. His parents, Mario and Regina, belonged to the large Italian community in the Argentine capital, Buenos Aires, and the family spoke Italian. They were **devout** Roman Catholics. Every night, the family said prayers before dinner. Their priest, Don Enrico Pozzoli, often joined them to eat. Many boys of Jorge's background became priests, but his parents wanted him to go to college. His mom hoped he would become a doctor and earn a good living. She did not want him to have to worry about money as she and his father had done.

QUICK FACTS

✿ Jorge Bergoglio decided as a teenager to become a priest.

✿ He joined a branch of the Catholic church called the Society of Jesus, or Jesuits.

A RELIGIOUS CALLING

When he was just 16, Jorge decided to become a priest. He was supported by his grandmother, Rosa, to whom he was very close, and Don Enrico, the family priest. However, his parents were worried and opposed the decision. Jorge was a soccer fanatic. How would he combine his love of soccer with his religious duties? They also knew that he would never be able to marry and have his own family. Catholic priests take a **vow** of **chastity**, which means they can't have children. However, Jorge would not change his mind.

In 1957, Jorge fell sick with a lung disease. He spent a month in hospital in great pain. During that time, he thought hard about being weak and unable to help himself. He became even more determined to become a priest and help other people. After having part of a lung removed, Jorge made a full recovery.

Jorge (left) with his younger brother.

BECOMING A PRIEST

In 1958, Jorge started his religious training. He was a trainee priest, or novice, in the Jesuit branch of the Catholic Church. He spent two years studying. His day started at 6:20 a.m. and ended at 10:30 p.m., with no free time between. Jorge was taught to think about his actions three times a day to see if there was anything he could have done better. Every now and then, a senior priest, called a novice master, called a meeting of the novices. As part of the process, he picked one novice and invited the other novices to criticize his behavior. When it was Jorge's turn, all the novices criticized him for being too serious.

Jorge was a smart and enthusiastic student.

In 1960, Jorge took his first vows of poverty, chastity, and **obedience** as a Jesuit priest. He vowed to obey God and the church, and to live simply. He was now a Jesuit priest, but he still needed many more years of study before he became an **ordained** priest, which gave him the authority to carry out religious ceremonies.

A TEACHING CAREER

In 1961, Jorge moved to neighboring Chile to continue his studies and to teach poor children. While he was there both his father, Mario, and Don Enrico passed away. The poverty Jorge saw in Chile shocked him. Children went to school hungry and without shoes. The future pope began to understand better how poverty affected people. When he returned to Argentina in 1963, he carried on teaching. This time, however, the pupils at his Jesuit school were from wealthy families. While he taught, Jorge continued his own studies and graduated with a degree in **philosophy**.

Buenos Aires has always been a city of contrasts between the rich and the poor.

CHANGE IN THE AIR

While Jorge studied and taught during the 1960s, he was among many Catholics who realized that the church needed to change. For centuries, it had been deeply **conservative**. All its services were held in Latin, a language that was no longer spoken. It did little to help the poor and needy. It also rejected the beliefs of other branches of Christianity.

Don Enrico Pozzoli was a role model for the young priest.

In 1965, Catholic leaders from around the world met in Rome, Italy, to discuss change. They decided to allow church services to be held in everyday languages. In addition, although the Catholic church had always claimed to be the only "true" religion, it now agreed to work with other religions to increase **tolerance** and understanding. Jorge welcomed these changes. He believed they would bring the church closer to the people.

As a young priest, Jorge saw great wealth and great poverty in Chile and Argentina.

ORDAINED AT LAST

In December 1969, Jorge was finally ordained as a Jesuit priest. Soon afterward, he was made head of the Department of Theology and Philosophy at the Jesuit College where he taught. In 1973, he took his final vows in the Jesuit order and the church promoted him to the position of Jesuit Provincial Superior. This meant he was now in charge of all the Jesuits in Argentina and neighboring Uruguay. He was now 36 years old. His experience of many years teaching and traveling overseas to learn languages and further his studies was about to be put to the test at home in Buenos Aires.

Jorge decided he would use his position to try and help as many people as possible. He worked with other Jesuits in the poorest neighborhoods of Buenos Aires and other cities. He opened new churches in city slums. He tried to help the poor, the sick, and those in prison. He thought the church often ignored such people.

Jorge (back row, second from left) remained close to his family.

The JESUITS

Also known as the Society of Jesus, the Jesuit order is the largest order within the Catholic church. It has more than 17,000 members.

The order was founded in the 1500s by a Spanish soldier named Ignatius of Loyola. In 1521, Ignatius was wounded in battle. As he recovered, he started to read about Jesus and the saints. The more he read, the more he was convinced he had to change the way he lived. One night, he saw the Virgin Mary in a vision, and decided to dedicate his life to serving God.

In 1548, Ignatius wrote a book about how to live a **spiritual** life. He said that people must serve God, live simply, give up power, and help others.

A Jesuit **seminary** in Ukraine. Jesuits taught students around the world.

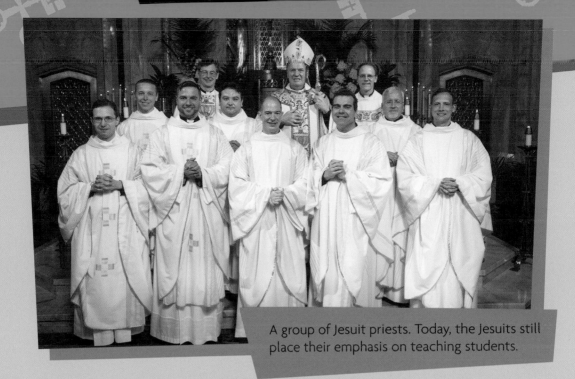

A group of Jesuit priests. Today, the Jesuits still place their emphasis on teaching students.

Ignatius said people should have the same discipline and **loyalty** as soldiers. They would be "soldiers of Christ." Ignatius's teachings attracted followers who founded the Society of Jesus. In 1622, Ignatius was made a saint.

The Jesuits wanted to help the Catholic church reconnect with ordinary people. They placed great importance on education. They set up many Jesuit schools and colleges. Many of these schools and colleges still operate today.

Ignatius of Loyola (center) and his companions take their vows at the founding of the Society of Jesus.

A Religious
CAREER

Jorge's career faltered when he found himself disagreeing with other members of the church during the 1970s and 1980s.

During the 1960s, Argentina's government was taken over by military **dictators**. For the next two decades, the military ran the country. During that time, many opponents of the government were killed or disappeared. This period was known as the "Dirty War." Other Jesuits accused Jorge of not speaking out against the military rulers. They also accused him of not working as part of a team and ignoring advice. Some Jesuit priests wanted to make a stand against the government, but Jorge thought it was a better idea to keep quiet. Later, he admitted he was wrong.

QUICK FACTS

* Jorge upset many people when he seemed not to stand up to Argentina's harsh government.

* He later gained a reputation for caring for the poor.

17

A DIFFICULT TIME

Jorge continued in his position as a Jesuit Provincial Superior until 1980. He had made himself very unpopular with his fellow Jesuits. They did not realize that he worked secretly to help people who were in danger of being arrested by the military dictators, or junta. Jorge had hidden them at the Jesuit headquarters and arranged for their escape to Europe. If he had been found out, he would have been sent to prison or executed.

At the time, nobody knew any of this. Jorge's enemies within the Jesuits decided he should not stay in his position. Instead, they said he must go back to studying philosophy. Jorge went to Germany to finish his **thesis** before returning to Argentina, where he studied at a number of universities.

The leaders of the junta were the heads of the armed services.

Argentines protest the disappearance of young people in the 1970s.

TESTING HIS FAITH

In 1990, Jorge's seniors in the Jesuit order sent him to a Jesuit seminary in Córdoba, in central Argentina. He was forbidden from carrying out many of the duties of a priest. He could not teach students or say Mass. He could not even make a phone call without asking permission. He was being punished for what people saw as his refusal to stand up to the military. One of the vows a Jesuit priest takes is of obedience to the order. Jorge's obedience was being tested. While he was in Córdoba, he managed to complete his thesis and spent a lot of time thinking about his Christian faith.

Citizens in Buenos Aires still create tributes to remember the Disappeared.

A NEW ROLE

In 1992, the church decided that Jorge had been punished enough. It asked him to help the **archbishop** of Buenos Aires run the city's Catholic churches. The city had a population of three million people. Almost one third of them lived in poverty. The city had many problems. There were few jobs, pay was low, and crime was high.

During the years in Córdoba, Jorge had thought a lot about how he could do things better in the future. Now he had the chance to put those thoughts into action. He decided that he would no longer make decisions alone. He would ask for advice and take it.

In Buenos Aires, Jorge worked to improve conditions in the slums and often visited them himself. Although the slums could be dangerous for outsiders, Jorge never took a bodyguard with him. He always walked everywhere, because it gave him a chance to talk to everyone he met. He raised money to build schools and **soup kitchens**, so even the very poorest people would receive an education and have something to eat.

ARCHBISHOP OF BUENOS AIRES

Six years later, in 1998, Jorge became the archbishop of Buenos Aires. His new position entitled him to live in a large house, wear silk robes, and travel in luxury. But none of this interested him. Jorge only wanted to help other people, so he continued to live in a small apartment, cook his own meals, and use public transportation.

As archbishop, Jorge impressed people with his modest lifestyle.

Jorge (right) chats with a parishioner
on the subway in Buenos Aires.

Jorge set an example for other priests about how
the Catholic church should interact with people.
His popularity soared. In the city's slums, people
gave him the affectionate nickname of the "Dude."
As Argentina's economy collapsed during the late
1990s and early 2000s, Jorge started to speak out
against how the government was handling the
economy. He said more should be done to help
ordinary people. His efforts to help the situation
gained him many admirers. News about his work
traveled all the way to Rome.

Jorge (right) embraces Pope John Paul II at the ceremony to make him a cardinal.

A CARDINAL

Pope John Paul II was a reformer, like Jorge. He wanted to use his position in the church to help the poor and vulnerable in society. When he heard about Jorge's work in Argentina, he was impressed. In 2001, the pope made Jorge a cardinal. Only the pope is able to appoint a cardinal. The position is very important. Cardinals are the highest-ranking officials in the Catholic church after the pope himself. There are 120 cardinals at any one time. One of their jobs is to gather in Rome when a new pope has to be elected.

The cardinals are the senior Roman Catholic officials from around the world.

The Dirty WAR

During the 1960s, Argentina was taken over by a series of military dictatorships. The leaders of the army, air force, and navy formed a ruling group known as the junta.

In 1976, the junta became intolerant of opposition. Argentines who spoke out against its brutal and **authoritarian** rule were "disappeared." They were taken away and never seen again. The missing people became known as *Los Desaparecidos* ("the Disappeared"). They were mainly people opposed to military rule.

Their families believed the Disappeared were murdered by the junta's death squads, who killed thousands of people by throwing them out of military airplanes into the Atlantic Ocean.

The faces of some of the Disappeared.

Mothers of the Disappeared still march in Buenos Aires in protest.

The period from 1976 until 1983 is known as the Dirty War. Human rights organizations estimate that death squads killed as many as 30,000 Argentines. In 1977, mothers of people who had been disappeared began to march in the Plaza de Mayo in front of the president's palace in Buenos Aires. They marched there every week until 2006 to draw attention to their lost children. Their protests helped to awaken international awareness of the brutal regime and helped bring it to an end. Although Jorge Bergoglio was criticized for not taking a stand against the junta, it later became known that he was helping its opponents to escape.

General Jorge Videla, president of Argentina from 1976, cracked down on all opposition.

25

A New
POPE

Pope John Paul II's recognition of Jorge's work with the poor in the slums of Buenos Aires was the start of a new part of Jorge's life.

Jorge had to travel to Rome for a ceremony in which the pope presents a new cardinal with the traditional red silk robes of office. Jorge went to Rome alone. He told his family and friends to save their airfare and give the money to **charity**. He also decided to wear his red robes only when he had to. They were not needed for his work. When he returned to Buenos Aires from Rome, he refused to move to his official residence. He stayed in his apartment. It was clear the new cardinal, now officially known as the priest of Saint Robert Bellarmino, was doing things differently.

QUICK FACTS

❖ As a cardinal, Jorge became well known for rejecting a life of luxury and privilege.

❖ In 2005, he traveled to Rome to take part in the election of Pope Benedict XVI.

A DIFFERENT CARDINAL

As a cardinal, Jorge carried on with his daily life. He continued to work in the slums of Buenos Aires. He visited the sick and dying in the hospital and spent time comforting them. In 2001, he made headlines across the world when he was photographed washing the feet of people suffering from the disease **HIV/AIDS**.

Jorge wearing the red robes of a cardinal.

In the church, washing people's feet is a sign of humility commemorating Jesus Christ's last supper with his disciples. In 1998, shortly after he became archbishop of Buenos Aires, Jorge had sent one of his junior bishops to the cathedral to carry out a traditional ceremony of the washing of feet on Maundy Thursday, part of the Easter celebrations.

Jorge and a fellow churchman visit a poor area of Buenos Aires.

While his junior archbishop went to the cathedral, Jorge headed to a local public hospital, where he washed the feet of 12 HIV/AIDS patients. Then he took the bus to the local jail, where he washed the feet of 12 prisoners. Jorge was making the point that the church's job was to help those who were in need. He wanted to focus on people who felt that society had forgotten them. He carried this focus throughout his later career, first as cardinal, and then as pope.

A CHURCH IN CRISIS

Jorge understood the need for a strong and unified Catholic church. He worked hard to bring together the Jesuit order, which had split into opposing groups. He had learned from experience that he needed to work with other church members and not to make all his decisions alone. His new way of working made the church a powerful force in Argentina. It challenged the government and provided real hope for many Argentines.

RESISTING CHANGE

Elsewhere, however, the Catholic church was in worse shape. A number of scandals had seriously damaged its reputation and image in the world.

Even as archbishop, Jorge made time to follow the Argentine soccer team.

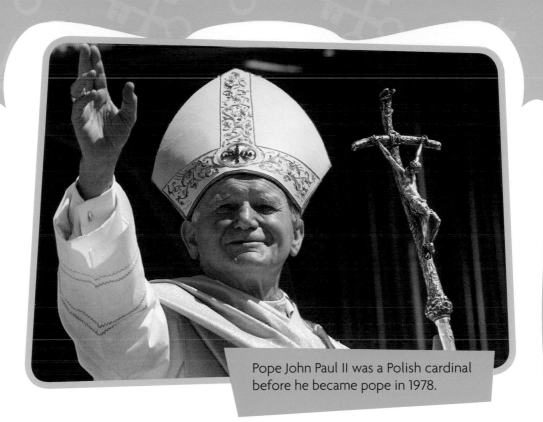
Pope John Paul II was a Polish cardinal before he became pope in 1978.

The pope, John Paul II, worked hard to make the church more **inclusive**, but he faced opposition from those inside the church who did not want change. The pope wanted to change the church's traditional refusal to allow women to hold office. Other religions let women become ministers. Some **Protestant** churches had changed to allow this. The Pope's opponents refused to consider the change. The Catholic church also continued to ban divorce or gay marriage. As a result of these conservative views, thousands of people were leaving the Catholic church each year.

ALL CHANGE

On April 2, 2005, Pope John Paul II died. His attempts to modernize the church had made him one of the most popular popes of recent times. Two weeks later, Jorge and the other cardinals went to Rome to elect a new pope in a ceremony known as the papal conclave.

Pope Benedict replaced Pope John Paul II in 2005.

On April 18, 2005, the new pope appeared on the balcony of St. Peter's Basilica in Vatican City to greet the huge crowds waiting to see him. The new pope was one of the oldest popes ever elected. Cardinal Joseph Ratzinger of Germany was 78 years old when he became the 265th pope. He chose to be called Benedict, and became Pope Benedict XVI. Although the voting procedure to elect a new pope is secret, Jorge discovered that he had come second in the cardinals' vote. There had never been a pope from the Americas.

CARRYING ON

Jorge returned to Buenos Aires happy. He had not wanted to become pope. He still had work to finish in Argentina before he planned to retire at age 75. Jorge carried on working in the slums, visiting the sick, and speaking out on subjects he thought were important for the church. He argued that it was time for the Catholic church to allow gay people to marry in **civil ceremonies**. He also thought that children of parents who had not married should be able to be **baptized** in church. Increasingly, people agreed with Jorge. He had become a very popular leader.

Jorge spent much of his time working in the crowded slums of Buenos Aires.

Papal ELECTIONS

The election of a new pope follows strict guidelines, some of which are hundreds of years old. The College of Cardinals elects the pope.

Up to 120 cardinals are able to vote in the papal conclave (cardinals over 80 years old are excluded). They all attend the conclave in the headquarters of the Catholic church, St. Peter's Basilica in Vatican City. The cardinals cannot vote anywhere else. The cardinals gather in the famous Sistine Chapel in the papal palace to vote. During the conclave they have no contact with the outside world. Any cardinal may be elected pope if he receives a two-thirds majority of the votes.

Cardinals gather for the papal conclave in 2013.

The ceiling of the Sistine Chapel was painted by the artist Michelangelo in the 1500s.

The voting takes place in rounds. In each round, cardinals make speeches supporting candidates and a secret vote is held. After each round, the candidate with fewest votes is elminated. After each vote, smoke is released from the Sistine Chapel chimney. Black smoke means that no pope has been chosen. White smoke indicates a successful election. There is no time limit on the process. In the 1200s, it once took almost three years to choose a new pope!

White smoke marks Jorge's election on March 13, 2013. He received 76 votes out of 115.

Leading the World's
CATHOLICS

A surprise announcement from Rome catapulted Jorge from the slums of Buenos Aires to the Vatican.

To widespread shock, Pope Benedict XVI announced on February 11, 2103, that he was stepping down. It was the first time since 1294 that a pope had resigned. But Pope Benedict was 85 years old and was in poor health. In addition, revelations of scandals continued to rock the Catholic church. Benedict believed the church needed a strong leader who could guide it through a period of crisis. For the second time in a decade, it was necessary to elect a new pope. Jorge went to Rome to attend the papal conclave, along with other cardinals from around the world.

QUICK FACTS

❀ Jorge became Pope Francis in March 2013.

❀ He introduced reforms in the Catholic church, which upset some traditionalists.

37

A NEW POPE

After two days of deliberation, on March 13, 2013, the cardinals elected Jorge Bergoglio as the 266th pope. He was the first pope from Latin America, which is home to about 40 percent of the world's 1.2 billion Catholics. Jorge was also the first Jesuit to become pope. Jorge was now 76 years old. He chose the pontifical name Francis, after the 13th-century saint Francis of Assisi. Saint Francis had dedicated his life to helping the poor and vulnerable. He was famous for his love of animals.

Saint Francis was the founder of the Franciscan order of monks.

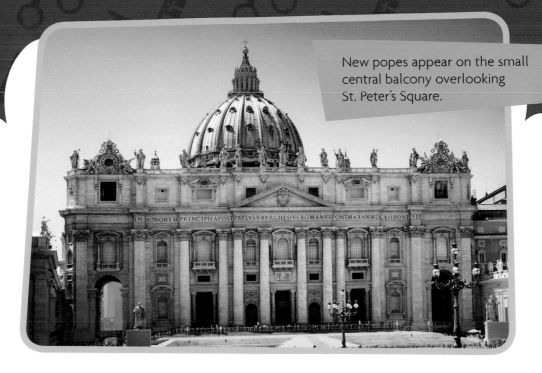

New popes appear on the small central balcony overlooking St. Peter's Square.

A VERY DIFFERENT POPE

It was soon clear that Francis intended to be a different kind of pope. When he appeared on the balcony of St. Peter's, he asked the crowd to bless him instead of blessing the crowd, as popes normally did. Francis rode the bus with the cardinals to his celebratory dinner, instead of taking his papal limousine. And he ate with the cardinals instead of sitting alone at the head table. Francis also announced that he would not use the luxurious papal apartments in the Vatican but instead would live in a simple house used for visiting priests. Some people criticized the pope for not showing the church enough respect. However, many others found this a refreshing change.

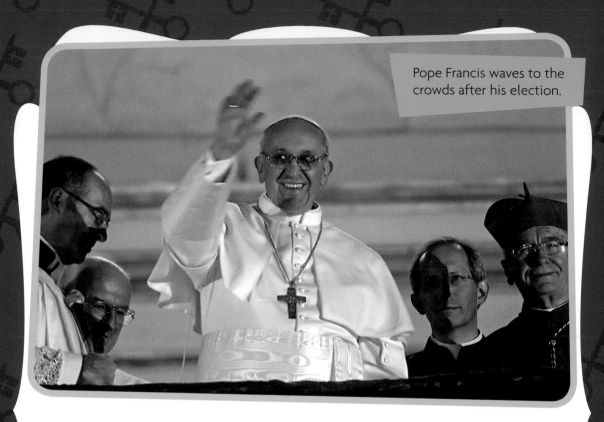

Pope Francis waves to the crowds after his election.

SETTING HIS OWN AGENDA

The new pope understood that he had to deal with the immediate problems facing the Catholic church. Among the scandals that had affected the church were rumors of corruption at the Vatican Bank, which held hundreds of millions of dollars belonging to the church. Francis quickly set about reforming the way the bank operated. He fired most of the bank's officers and replaced them with people he trusted. He also announced that the bank's accounts would now be available for everyone to examine.

REFORM IN THE VATICAN

Next, Francis dealt with the Curia. These were the 3,000 people on the staff in the Vatican. Francis believed the Curia was too conservative and reluctant to reform. He felt they tried to control his communications with the public. To show he intended to change, Francis even started to answer his own phone. When people called the Vatican, they were startled to find themselves talking to the Pope himself. To reach as many of his followers as possible directly, Francis set up his own Twitter and Facebook accounts.

Enthusiastic Catholics welcome the pope to an open-air mass.

INTERNATIONAL PEACEMAKER

At the end of 2013, *Time* magazine put Pope Francis on its front cover as their person of the year. Francis continued to work hard. One of his jobs was to act as a go-between in secret **negotiations** between the United States and Cuba, which had broken off **diplomatic** relations in 1961. After 18 months of negotiations, it was announced on Francis's 78th birthday, December 17, 2014, that the two countries were restoring communication. President Barack Obama and Cuba's president Raul Castro thanked Francis for his involvement. He was nominated for the 2014 Nobel Peace Prize, though he did not win.

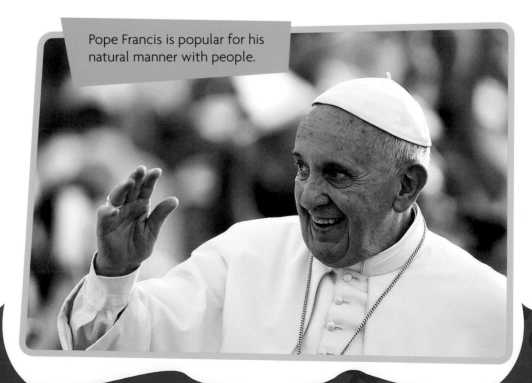

Pope Francis is popular for his natural manner with people.

A BUSY MAN

Pope Francis continued his involvement with political issues. He tried to help **refugees** from a war in Syria, for example. He also became involved in fighting **climate change**. In 2015, he wrote a 184-page encyclical—a letter to all church bishops— about the threat of climate change.

Pope Francis meets US president Barack Obama in 2014.

Pope Francis was not afraid to take on controversial causes. He was the first pope to speak in support of gay people and not to condemn women who have abortions. He also said he believed in evolution and supported the **Big Bang** theory. Many traditionalists feel that both of these beliefs contradict the Bible. Pope Francis continues to travel to meet Catholics around the world and promote his message that the church will only survive if it becomes more inclusive.

Timeline

1936 • Born to Italian immigrant parents in Buenos Aires, Argentina, on December 17.

1957 • Falls seriously sick with pneumonia. Spends a month in the hospital, where he becomes determined to become a priest.

1958 • Joins the Society of Jesus, or Jesuits, as a novice.

1960 • Takes his first vows as a Jesuit.

1961 • Begins studying philosophy at the San Miguel seminary in Buenos Aires. He spends the first two years of the course teaching in Chile.

1963 • Returns to Argentina, where he continues his work as a teacher.

1965 • Catholic leaders introduce reforms to try to update the church. Jorge supports the changes.

1969 • Is ordained as a priest on December 13.

1973 • Becomes the senior Jesuit in charge of Argentina and Uruguay.

1976 • The military junta in Argentina begins a "dirty war" against its political opponents.

1990 • The church sends Jorge to a Jesuit seminary in Córdoba, Argentina.

1992 • Recalled to Buenos Aires and made a bishop, Jorge runs the city's churches.

1998 • Becomes archbishop of Buenos Aires.

2001	• Is made a cardinal by Pope John Paul II.
2005	• After the death of John Paul II, takes part in the papal conclave to elect Pope Benedict XVI.
2013	• Pope Benedict announces his decision to retire in February.
	• On March 13, Jorge is elected as Pope Francis, the first Jesuit and the first South American to hold the office.
	• Appoints a group of cardinals to reform the Curia.
	• In December the pope is announced as *Time* magazine's person of the year.
2014	• In March, Pope Francis meets President Barack Obama in the Vatican.
	• The pope arranges a political agreement between the United States and Cuba.
2015	• Travels to the United States to address Congress and the United Nations.
2016	• Becomes the first pope to have an Instagram account. He gains a million followers within 12 hours.

KEY PUBLICATIONS

❧ *The Joy of the Gospel* (2014)

❧ *The Church of Mercy* (2014)

❧ *Dear Pope Francis: The Pope Answers Letters from Children Around the World* (2016)

❧ *The Joy of Love: On Love in the Family* (2016)

❧ *Embracing the Way of Jesus* (2017)

Glossary

archbishop The chief bishop responsible for a large area.

authoritarian Enforcing rules without flexibility.

baptized Given a name and made a member of the church.

Big Bang The theory that the universe came into being in a single explosion.

charity An organization that helps those in need.

chastity Not taking part in sexual relations.

civil ceremonies Nonreligious marriage ceremonies.

climate change The process by which human activity changes Earth's atmosphere.

conservative Having traditional values and being reluctant to changes.

controversy A long public disagreement and argument.

devout Very religious.

dictators Rulers with total control in a country.

diplomatic Concerned with relations between countries.

HIV/AIDS A disease that is often fatal.

inclusive Welcoming everyone.

loyalty Support for a country, individual, or cause.

negotiations Talks to resolve a dispute between two sides.

obedience Submission to someone else's authority.

ordained Made a minister of the church.

papal Related to the pope.

philosophy The study of the nature of knowledge and life.

Protestant A branch of Christianity that broke away from the Catholic church in the 1500s.

refugees People who have been forced to leave their homes by violence, war, or persecution.

seminary A college for training future priests.

soup kitchens Places where free food is served to the poor.

spiritual Related to the human spirit or soul.

thesis A long essay written by a university student.

tolerance Willingness to coexist peacefully with other people's opinions or beliefs.

vow A solemn promise to do certain things.

Further Resources

Books

Castro, Emanuel. *Pope Francis.* Chicago: Capstone Press, 2017.

Machajewski, Sarah. *Pope Francis: The People's Pontiff.* New York: Rosen Publishing Group, 2014.

Nanji, Shenaaz. *Vatican City.* New York: Av2 by Weigl, 2014.

Pope Francis. *Dear Pope Francis: The Pope Answers Letters from Children Around the World.* Chicago: Loyola Press, 2016.

Putra, Dede. *Who Is Pope Francis?* New York: Grosset and Dunlap, 2017.

Websites

Biography.com
www.biography.com/people/ pope-francis-21152349
A biography of Pope Francis, with a short video.

CNN
edition.cnn.com/2013/03/14/ world/pope-francis-fast-facts/ index.html
Fast facts about Pope Francis from CNN, with a timeline of his papacy.

The Fact Site
www.thefactsite.com/2015/10/ pope-francis-facts.html
20 interesting facts about Pope Francis.

The Papacy
people.howstuffworks.com/ papacy.htm
How Stuff Works pages about the papacy and the Roman Catholic church.

Publisher's note to educators and parents: Our editors have carefully reviewed these websites to ensure that they are suitable for students. Many websites change frequently, however, and we cannot guarantee that a site's future contents will continue to meet our high standards of quality and educational value. Be advised that students should be closely supervised whenever they access the Internet.

Index